The Haunting of Zona Heaster Shue

The Greenbrier Ghost Chronicles

Nancy Richmond
and
Misty Murray-Walkup

Cover Art by
Misty Murray-Walkup

http://mistymurraywalkupgallery.webstarts.com
Laurel Creek Mountain Art on facebook

A Richmond Book Publication

About the Authors

Nancy Richmond is a retired Greenbrier County Judge, a certified genealogist, a newspaper and magazine columnist, and an award winning author of over 30 books. Nancy is a lifelong resident of Greenbrier County. She currently resides with her husband Charles in Historic Lewisburg, West Virginia.

Misty Murray-Walkup is a Greenbrier County artist, author and book illustrator. Her paintings have appeared in Carnegie Hall, and have been juried into Tamarack in West Virginia. They can be found in public and private galleries around the world. Misty is a member of the art group 'Greenbrier Artists' and was a featured artist at the Foundation for Appalachian Advancement. A collection of her paintings (in book form) are on display at the Library of Congress in Washington, DC. Misty operates the Laurel Creek Mountain Art Gallery at Orient Hill, West Virginia, where she resides with her family.

Contents

Foreword

The legend of Zona Heaster Shue, whose ghost appeared to her mother and revealed that she was murdered by her husband, and whose story was used to convict that husband in a court of law, is well known to the public. There are several books dedicated to the tale, as well as numerous short stories and websites. Most of them vary greatly in content and contain conflicting information about the incident. In an effort to create an accurate account of the event, the authors have gathered all the verifiable evidence available to produce this volume. That evidence is included in the 'Documentation' section at the back of the book. {Please note that some birth and death dates and the spelling of some names may vary in the marriage, death, and census records}.

The cover art was painted from a photograph of Zona and Trout on their wedding day. Zona's dress had a high stiff collar. According to witnesses, it is the dress she was buried in and was wearing when she appeared to her mother as a ghost.

The most remarkable part of the story - other than the ghost herself - is that during the trial of Erasmus 'Trout' Shue, the testimony of the ghost Zona Heaster Shue (as related by her mother) was not objected to by either the prosecution or the defense. Consequently, the account was not declared inadmissable by the judge, making it the only court case in US history where a ghost helped to convict a suspect in a murder trial.

A Ghostly Encounter

When we set out to write this book, we had no idea that we would experience what seems to have been a paranormal encounter with Zona Heaster Shue's ghost. But that is exactly what happened. Misty wanted to paint a portrait of Zona for the book's cover. There is a wedding photo of Zona, wearing the dress she was both married and buried in. However, the photo is in black and white, so there is no way to know what color her dress was.

While discussing the matter, we printed out a copy of the wedding picture of Zona, to be used as a reference for the portrait. The printer was set for black and white copies, so we were stunned when the lower portion of the picture (just covering the paper up to the neck of the dress) came out wine red! Needless to say, that is the color Misty chose for the dress.

None of the other dozen or so documents we printed that day had any discoloration, and we truly feel that Zona was communicating with us. She may have wanted to tell us that her dress was red, or perhaps she was trying to prove to a new generation that she had indeed been murdered by her husband more than a hundred years ago.

Nancy Richmond   *Misty Murray-Walkup*

5

Zona Heaster

Chapter One
Zona Heaster

Elva Zona Heaster was born around 1875 to parents Jacob Hedges Heaster and Mary Jane (Robinson) Heaster. Zona was the couple's second child and only daughter, as she had one older and five younger brothers.

The Heaster family owned one of a dozen farms which lay along the path of the Midland Trail in Greenbrier County, West Virginia, located deep in the heart of the Appalachian Mountains. The trail meandered past Little Sewell Mountain some fifteen miles east of the county seat of Lewisburg, and west ten miles to the town of Rupert. The closest community, Livesay's Mill, was only a few miles from the farm, and was where the Heaster family regularly shopped and sold the eggs and vegetables they produced on their farm.

Zona was a beautiful child, with long dark hair and soft brown eyes that could be dancing with mischief one moment and raining down tears the next, for she had by all accounts a tender heart. Because she was the only girl in the family she was doted on by her parents and brothers, but also carefully watched over, lest some harm should come to her.

Even with the relative isolation of farm life in the late 1800s, Zona and her brothers were happy children, helping with the farm work and playing together in the nearby woodlands, meadows and creeks that surrounded their home. The Heasters lived within walking distance of the only two official buildings in the area. These were the little log cabin Nickell Schoolhouse and the Soule Methodist Chapel, which was organized in 1849 and named after the local circuit rider preacher. Zona's mother Mary was deeply religious and took her children to church regularly.

One of Zona's jobs on the farm was to collect the eggs from the chicken house each morning, and carry them into the barn to be washed and placed in wicker baskets. Then she and her mother would load them in the wagon and drive them into Livesay's Mill to be bartered or sold to the grocer for other items that they needed.

Livesay's Mill was named for the large grist mill that straddled Milligan Creek. The wooden structure was the hub of the farming community, for it was there that the residents had their corn and wheat ground and bagged for resale. Besides the mill, the town boasted a general store, a church, a sheriff's office, a post office, a doctor's office, a school house, a blacksmith shop and a boarding house. Around the shops were a cluster of one and two story homes. Zona never tired of the hustle and bustle that animated the little country town, and she loved watching the huge wood wheel of the mill as it endlessly rotated into and out of the creek.

By the time Zona was sixteen, her parents considered her old enough and capable enough to harness one of the work horses to the wagon and load it with the items that needed to be taken to the general store and traded. The arrangement allowed her mother to stay home and care for her younger brothers and tend to the daily farm chores. Sometimes one of the boys would accompany Zona into town, but since they were needed in the fields (especially her older brother) she often made the trip alone.

It was while on one of her visits into town that Zona met a young man named George Woldridge, the son of a Fayette County farmer. George, who was a few years older than Zona, was working in Livesay's Mill as a laborer, and before long they were meeting on a regular basis when Zona came to town. The young people soon fell in love.

In the spring of 1895, Zona had to reveal to her parents that she was expecting a baby. After much prayer and soul searching everyone agreed that the young man was not able to support a wife and child at that time, and it was decided that there would be no marriage. Instead, George promised to pay support for the baby, and visit it regularly.

On the 29th day of November Dr. Leancy Rupert was called to the Heaster farm. He was the son of Dr. Cyrus Rupert, for whom the nearby town of Rupert was named. After several hours, Zona gave birth to a little boy. The infant lived only a short time. Consequently, he was not christened or given a name in the courthouse records. The baby was buried on the family farm rather than in the church graveyard, as his parents were not married. Zona was devastated at the loss of her child, and was inconsolable for months. She and George Woldridge ended their relationship, and the following year he married a young woman from Virginia.

As the long winter passed, Mary Heaster prayed ceaselessly for her suffering daughter, asking God to take Zona's sorrow and shame away and allow her to have peace once more. Eventually Zona seemed to recover from the ordeal, although she was never the happy, carefree girl that she once had been.

Trout Shue

Chapter Two
Trout Shue

Erasmus Stribbling Trout Shue was born around 1861 to parents Jacob Thomas Shue and Elizabeth Virginia (Cook) Shue. Everyone called the little boy Trout, and because he had a delicate constitution, he was 'spoilt' by his mother and siblings. Trout saw little of his father when he was small, because Jacob Shue was a Confederate soldier during the Civil War and did not return home until 1865.

After the war, the Shue family lived at Droop Mountain in Pocahontas County, where Trout's father returned to his pre-war occupation as a blacksmith. Trout had eight brothers and sisters, which was an average family in West Virginia at the time. As a child, Trout loved telling stories and being the center of attention. He also had a dominant personality and a hot temper, which sometimes landed him in trouble.

When he grew to adulthood, Trout worked with his father at the blacksmith shop. By 1880, Jacob Shue had amassed a large amount of money, and was one of the most prominent men in the county. Trout, a handsome and powerfully built young man, took advantage of the good fortune of his family and courted many of the most eligible young women of his acquaintance.

Trout eventually settled on Ellen (Allie) Estelline Cutlip, the daughter of James and Emily Cutlip. Allie was a pretty young girl from Greenbrier County and Trout was her first beau. The two married on Christmas Eve in 1885. The union was not a loving one, and on more than one occasion Trout abused his young bride.

Allie stayed with her husband in spite of the fact that he was not a good provider. Trout often spent days away from home, which he refused to account for. Within a year of their marriage, Allie became pregnant. In February of 1887, she delivered a daughter that the couple named Girta Lucretia Shue.

After the birth of the baby, Trout's actions became even more erratic. He was gone from home much of the time, and was not making enough money to support his family. In March of 1888, just after Girta turned a year old, Trout told Allie to pack her belongings, take the baby and get out of his house. When she refused to do so, he threw everything she owned outside, gathered up his belongings and left.

Trout spent the rest of the year finding work wherever he could. He either would not or could not turn to his father for help, and his situation became desperate.

In the fall of 1888, Trout Shue was arrested for stealing a horse from a man on Droop Mountain, and was taken to Hillsboro for a preliminary hearing before the Justice of the Peace, the Honorable Justice Kennison. Since he could not make bail, Trout was put in the local jail, where he waited until April 3, 1889 to be tried.

Shue's trial did not take long, because he pled guilty to the charges and was automatically convicted of being a horse thief. He was given a two year sentence in the State Penitentiary, which was located in the town of Moundsville in Marshall

County, some two hundred miles from Hillsboro.

Eight days later, on April 11, Trout Shue was remanded to the Moundsville prison. Built in 1876, the massive Gothic style stone fortress looked more like a medieval castle than a prison. Trout was led to the warden's office, where he was assigned his prison number - 1817. An identification sheet for him was filled out by the prison administrator.

The physical record described Trout as being a white man of medium build and height, with blue eyes. He had a large scar on his left ankle. It was noted that he was an educated man. Trout was then taken to the cell that would be his home for the next twenty-two months.

All of the healthy inmates at the

prison were assigned jobs which they were required to perform each day. These included working in the wagon shop, bakery, hospital, tailor shop or blacksmith shop. Trout was sent to the latter, because he had worked as a blacksmith for much of his life and knew the trade well.

Allie Shue took advantage of Trout's incarceration to begin divorce proceedings, knowing he would not be able to harass or intimidate her from his prison cell. The divorce hearing took place in Greenbrier County. Allie told the court that *"He without any cause abandoned and deserted me. He moved out when Girtie was about a year old."* On November 5, 1889, the divorce was granted.

Trout left the Moundsville prison on December 20, 1890, having been released two months early for good behavior. He returned to the Droop Mountain area of Pocahontas County, where he worked either as a farm laborer or a blacksmith during the next four years. Trout made little effort to contact his ex-wife Allie or to see his child.

In 1894, Trout met Lucy Ann Tritt, the daughter of Isaac and Elizabeth Tritt. Lucy was only sixteen at the time. Trout and Lucy courted throughout the spring, and on June 23 they were married in Greenbrier County by Pastor G. O. Homan. A few months later Trout found work in Hillsboro in Pocahontas County, and the newlyweds moved into an old house near his job.

The winter of 1894-1895 was unusually severe in West Virginia, and snowstorms were frequent. On February 11, Trout claimed that he had climbed onto the roof of his house to repair damage caused by the storms. He said that he was throwing old bricks off the roof as he replaced them with new ones. Just as Lucy was bringing him a drink of water, Trout tossed one of the bricks off the roof, hitting her on the head. Shue went for the local doctor, who pronounced that Lucy had died from the injury. When the sheriff questioned Trout, he insisted that her death was an accident.

There was no clear evidence of what had taken place at the time of Lucy's death, as there were no witnesses, although many of her family members suspected foul play and brought up the fact that her husband was a convicted felon. Eventually, the investigation ended and Trout was not charged with killing Lucy, his wife of just eight months.

As soon as the weather permitted, Lucy Ann Shue was buried in the Whiting Cemetery on Droop Mountain. Trout Shue showed no sorrow for Lucy's death, and continued on with his life. He often told friends that the loss of his first two wives did not upset him, because he believed it was his destiny to have at least seven wives before he died.

Zona and Trout Shue

Chapter Three
Zona and Trout

The loss of her child and of her relationship with George devastated Zona. She continued to live on the farm with her parents, and became very close to her mother Mary. The two were sometimes mistaken for sisters, and had very similar personalities. Mary worried about Zona and prayed she would find a good man to marry and have a family of her own.

By the spring of 1896, Zona had started to show an interest in the outside world again, attending church, visiting friends and going into Livesay's Mill to deliver goods to the general store. She often rode along with her older brother when he drove the wagon to town to buy wire and other supplies for the farm. It was during one of these trips that Zona first met the new blacksmith, who introduced himself as Edward Trout Shue. He had begun calling himself Edward when he was released from prison, hoping to distance himself from his past.

Trout had become a drifter in the Pocahontas/Greenbrier area after the death of his second wife, never staying in one place for more than a few months at a time. He had traveled to Livesay's Mill after hearing that Charlie Tuckwiller, the owner of the town's blacksmith shop, was seeking a new smithy.

Trout got the job, and rented an older two story house that had been the home of Will Livesay until he died. The house stood on a hill that was within walking distance of the blacksmith shop, and the path leading to it could easily be seen from the double doors of the building when they were open.

Zona was intrigued by Trout's good looks and loud, boisterous manner. Since his arrival, the blacksmith shop had become a meeting place for the young people of the town, and Zona looked forward to visiting it as often as possible. Her mother Mary was happy and relieved to see Zona in such high spirits, although she had no idea what had brought about the change.

When Mary finally met Trout while on a trip to town with her husband, she took an instant dislike to him. She felt that he was a braggart, and acted entirely too forward towards the young girls (some of them barely more than children) who gathered around the blacksmith whenever he was telling one of his tall tales. Neither did Mary like Trout's intimidating demeanor towards the young men in the crowd. When she learned that Zona had been secretly meeting with Trout, Mary was appalled. She begged her daughter not to see him again. Zona, however, would not heed her mother's wishes. When Trout suggested that they run off and get married, Zona packed some bags, taking all of her belongings, and left for town.

Zona did not wear white for their wedding, since everyone knew she had given birth to a child. Instead, she wore a dress she had made that summer. It was wine colored and had a high collar which was decorated with white lace. She braided her hair, weaving wild flowers and bright fall leaves into the braid and finishing it with a large bow. Trout was in high spirits, telling everyone that Zona was his third bride and bragging about what a wonderful future they were going to have. On October 20, 1896, she and Trout traveled to the county seat, where they were married by Rev. T. W. Brown at the Lewisburg Station Parsonage.

There was no wedding dinner after the ceremony, as was the custom in the area, since Zona's parents did not approve of the union and had not attended the service. Instead, Trout and Zona returned to Livesay's Mill and retrieved her meager belongings from the blacksmith shop where she had left them. Then they walked up the hill to the little house Trout was renting, excited to begin their married life.

House where Zona was Murdered

Chapter Four
Zona's Death

The weeks following the wedding were busy ones for Zona. She cleaned and polished everything in the old farm house, then spent time walking through the little town and talking with the residents. It was something she was unaccustomed to, since she had spent her life on her parent's isolated farm.

Zona's marriage was not the happy affair that she had expected it to be because Trout, once so funny and attentive, was now often surly and demanding. Adding complications to the situation was the fact that she was estranged from her family. Zona especially missed her mother, who refused to come to Trout's house to see her.

31

The one bright spot for Zona was that she thought she might be expecting a child. More than anything she wanted to be a mother, and Trout seemed to be equally happy at the idea of a baby. Dr. George Knapp, the town physician, had examined Zona and said that while it was too early to know for certain, she might indeed be with child. A baby, Zona was sure, would heal the breach with her family and make them accept her marriage to Trout.

So, although she had been feeling under the weather for a few days, it was with a happy heart that Zona began preparing a nice meal for Trout, who always expected to be fed as soon as he came home from work. She knew her husband would be cold, walking home in the deep snow and frigid temperature, and she did not want him to be cross with her for lying abed all day, even though she was not feeling well.

On January 23, Trout was extremely busy at the blacksmith shop. Although he usually walked home several times during the day, on that occasion he went across the street to the residence of Reuben and Martha Jones instead. Martha had been a slave on the nearby plantation of Morlunda before the Civil War, and was affectionately known as 'Aunt' Martha to her neighbors.

Trout asked Martha if her young son Anderson 'Andy' Jones could run up to his house and check on Zona because she was ill that morning and he was too busy to go. He also told Andy to gather the eggs for his wife and see if she needed him to bring anything from the store when he came home. Martha replied that Andy could go, but not until he

33

finished some work he had promised to do at Dr. Knapp's house. That seemed to anger Trout, but he agreed and went back to work. He checked several times to see if Andy had run the errand, but over an hour passed before the boy finally headed up the snowy hill to check on Zona.

Although he had visited the Shue house on numerous occasions to deliver messages or bring goods from the general store, Andy had a feeling that something was not right as he approached the front door that day. He saw a trail of what looked like blood drops on the front steps. After a moment, the boy knocked, but no one answered.

Andy slowly opened the door and followed the trail of blood into the dining room, where he saw Zona's lifeless body lying at the foot of the stairs.

Terrified, Andy ran home as fast as his legs would carry him. He was so frightened that at first he could not speak, but after his mother entreated him to tell her what was wrong, he finally managed to whisper a reply.

"All the doors were closed, and there was an air about the place I didn't like. There she was, stretched out on the floor, looking up at me through wide open eyes. She seemed to be laughing. I was frightened but still able to reach down and shake her. She was stiff and cold."

Horrified, Martha went with her son to break the news to Trout, who dropped what he was doing and ran to the house, followed by Martha Jones. They found Zona lying on the floor, just as Andy had reported. Her body was perfectly straight, with her feet together and with one hand by her side and the other draped across her body. Her head was inclined to one side. Trout ran to his wife, and after touching her, yelled at Martha to go and fetch the doctor.

It was after 2 p.m. when Dr. Knapp, who was also the Greenbrier County coroner, finally arrived at the Shue house. Trout had been busy in the time since Martha left him. He had carried his dead wife upstairs to the bedroom and washed her. Trout dressed her in the red gown she wore when they married, which had a high, stiff collar. He then closed her eyes and covered her face with a long black veil.

Because Zona had died so quickly, Dr. Knapp at first thought she might have had a heart attack, known in Appalachia as an 'everlasting faint'. But as he began to examine the body for any signs to support his theory, Trout became extremely agitated and even threatening towards him.

When the doctor tried to check Zona's neck, Trout lifted her upper body into his arms, cradling it against his chest and pushing the doctor away. Knapp, out of respect for Shue's grief and knowing that Zona may have been pregnant, declared that she must have died from complications of childbirth (miscarriage), and left the house.

News of the untimely death of Zona Shue spread quickly through the small town. Two men who were friends of the Heasters, Dick Watts and Lewis Stuart, volunteered to ride out to the farm and give the family the terrible news. It took several hours on the snow covered roads to reach the farm house, and the sun was already setting by the time the young men dismounted and knocked on the door. Mary began to wail when she heard of her daughter's untimely death, screaming "The devil has killed her!"

Watts and Stuart stayed at the farm for an hour, until everyone had calmed down. The family made arrangements with the two men to have Zona's body brought to their home, where they would hold the wake and then have her buried in the Soule Chapel cemetery the next day. Mary had no doubt that Trout would go along with their plans, since he did not own any property where he could bury his wife, nor was it likely that he had any money to pay for a funeral.

Zona's father gave Watts and Stuart enough cash to buy a coffin in town, and to have the body delivered the next day. He did not instruct the men to invite Trout to come with the body, but he knew his son-in-law would not allow the funeral to take place otherwise, so he left it to them to tell Trout what they thought best.

After the men departed, the family sat around the fireplace in silence, shocked and broken by the events of the day. It had only been three months since Zona left them, and now she would never return.

Church where Zona's Funeral was Held

Chapter Five
The Burial

The funeral carriage left Livesay's Mill early the next morning, the body of Zona Shue having been placed in a coffin from the Handley Undertaking Establishment just before dawn. No embalming had been done, which was not unusual at the time.

Trout would not leave the body, even for a moment, and rode next to the coffin in the hearse with his hand pressed against his dead wife's cheek. It took two hours for them to reach the Heaster farm, traveling slowly over the frozen and mud caked trails. The grief stricken Heaster family stood silently by as Trout and several neighbors carried the coffin into what once had been Zona's bedroom.

The custom of 'sitting up with the dead'

was an old one in the Appalachian Mountains, and numerous friends and neighbors spent the night on the farm, keeping vigil over the young woman's coffin. Everyone brought an offering of food for the mourners, although most of it went uneaten.

Trout Shue stayed close beside the casket, never allowing anyone to touch the body. He seemed determined to make himself into a tragic figure, as if to say it was he and not Zona that should be the center of the wake. Trout placed Zona's head on a deep pillow to support her neck on one side and lay a knotted sheet on the other side. He then wrapped a heavy scarf around her neck, saying that it was how Zona wanted to be buried. Although most of the family members and guests nodded off for a few hours of sleep through the night, Trout kept an alert vigil and never left the room.

The morning of the funeral was a somber one. Everyone was exhausted from grief and the dread of what was to come next. The coffin was carefully loaded into a wagon, and driven slowly to the Soule Chapel, which had been built almost fifty years earlier along the narrow trail that ran between the local farms. The family followed on foot behind the wagon, and only the sound of muffled sobs could be heard as they neared the church. The funeral was brief, with the preacher offering hope from the Bible that the family would be reunited with their lost loved one some glad day in paradise, and exhorting them to live a good life until that time came.

At the end of the service, Mary went forward and kissed her daughter's cold cheek. She then removed the pillow and sheet so that the coffin could be closed. A song was sung, then everyone except the immediate family left the church and headed to their respective homes. Only Mary, her husband and children and Trout Shue remained to watch as the narrow wooden coffin was lowered with ropes into a grave that had been dug the day before by church members.

Trout seemed relieved when the earth had been shoveled into the opening, covering the casket, and quickly headed back to town. Just before he left, Mary offered him the pillow and sheet he had placed in the coffin. Trout refused to take them, shrinking away from her outstretched hands as if she had offered him poison, so instead she placed them in the bag she had brought with her.

Zona's mother was one of the last to leave, and only left then at her husband's urging. Before she departed, Mary placed a wreath of fresh pine needles which she had made the night before on the cold earth that covered Zona's grave. It was the best that she could do, because there were no flowers to be had from the cold winter fields.

Mary Jane Heaster

Chapter Six
The Haunting

After the funeral, Mary Heaster could
not accept that Zona was gone. Her heart
seemed to be made of stone, as hard and cold
as her daughter had been when they lowered
her into the ground. Even more terrible than
the grief she felt, Mary was burdened by a
terrible fear that Zona had not died a natural
death at all, but had been killed in some
horrible way, and was crying out from the
grave for justice.

Every night after her husband and
children were asleep, Mary would go into her
daughter's room, lie down on the narrow bed,
and pray for God to show her some way to help
Zona be at peace. One night, as she finished
praying and opened her eyes, Mary saw a soft

light in the corner of the room that seemed to have no source. As she watched, the light grew larger and brighter until, with a thrill of horror, Mary saw the image of her daughter emerge and stand in front of her.

Zona was wearing the same dress she had been buried in and her expression was sad. But when the girl spoke her voice sounded so natural that Mary gathered her wits and asked her daughter how she had died.

The ghost told Mary that she had not felt well that day, and knowing that Trout would be coming home soon, she had set out a cold meal of bread, butter and fruit. But when Trout arrived, he was furious because there was no meat, and he had grabbed her possessions and thrown them in a basket and ruined them. Then he had choked her until she had blood running out of her mouth, killing her. Zona

told her mother to go and look behind the
house where Martha Jones lived, because that
was where Trout hid her bloody dress after he
had changed her clothes. She also said to look
in a field near the fence.

Mary listened in shock to Zona's terrible
story, and reached out to touch her daughter's
arm. To her surprise, Zona felt just as real as
she had when she was alive. Slowly, the ghost
faded away and the room was left in darkness.
Shaken and drained of emotion, Mary lay down
on her daughter's bed and fell into a deep sleep.

Zona's mother spent the following day in
a daze, but as night approached she realized that
her heart was not so heavy and that her sorrow
had turned to anger. She spoke to no one of the
vision she had seen, and went about her chores
as if nothing had happened.

As soon as her family went to bed that

night, Mary hurried into Zona's room and began to pray for God to let her see her daughter again. She had not been there long when the light once again appeared in the corner of the room, and Zona stepped out and stood before her mother.

Mary tried to talk with Zona, but the ghost did not answer any of her questions. Instead, she repeated the story she had told the night before, saying "Ma, he just took his hands and squeezed my neck off." Then, as she walked away, Zona turned her head completely around, looking sadly at her mother with her head facing the wrong way as she disappeared.

Mary ran from the room and got into bed beside her sleeping husband, terrified by what she had just seen. Still, she did not say anything to her family about Zona's visits. For the next two nights, Mary waited for Zona in her room, and on both nights Zona returned and told the same story.

Finally, feeling that her heart could not bear another such night, Mary stopped praying and told her family what she had seen. To her relief, they believed that Zona's ghost had come to her and agreed that Trout had killed her.

Encouraged, Mary began telling her neighbors that Zona had been murdered by Trout, and about the details the ghost had revealed to her as proof. Many of them did not like Trout, and convinced Mary to take her suspicions to the Greenbrier County Prosecuting Attorney, John Alfred Preston, who by chance lived not far from the house Trout Shue was renting in Livesay's Mill.

Mary was not a well educated woman, and as her wagon drove up to the entrance of the home of the prosecutor she was awed by the grandeur of the estate, but she did not allow it to deter her from her quest. She knew that Preston had graduated from Washington and Lee University, had been a member of the state senate and was the Ruling Elder in the Old Stone Presbyterian Church in Lewisburg. But she also knew that it was his job to investigate crimes and bring criminals to justice, so she bravely knocked at the door and waited to see him.

Mr. Preston was an elderly man, small of stature and bald, but he had a look of keen intelligence. He allowed Mary Heaster to tell her entire story before questioning her. As astounding as the tale was, he gave no hint of disbelief. He took down the names of anyone Mary thought might have information about the death, and promised that he would look into the matter.

After Mrs. Heaster departed, Preston

sent county deputies to question any residents who had knowledge of the incident. When Dr. Knapp admitted that Trout had been so angry and intimidating that he could not perform a proper examination, the prosecutor decided that an autopsy must be conducted in order to prove no foul play was involved in the death of Zona Heaster Shue.

Soule Chapel Cemetery

Chapter Seven

The Exhumation

Once it had been determined that the body of Zona Heaster Shue was to be exhumed and an autopsy performed, things moved quickly. Prosecuting Attorney Preston applied for and received a warrant to disturb a buried body. He also applied for a second warrant that was served on Trout Shue, to bind him over in the local jail until it was shown during the autopsy if a crime had been committed.

The weather had been very cold all through the month of February, so it was hoped that there would not be too much decomposition of the corpse, which would give those conducting the procedure a better chance of making a determination of the girl's death.

Just behind the Soule Chapel cemetery

where Zona was buried stood a small log cabin schoolhouse that would be the perfect place to conduct the autopsy. Classes at the Nickell schoolhouse were cancelled on the day of February 22, and three doctors were chosen to conduct an examination of the corpse.

The exhumation itself took several hours. It was hard work for volunteers to dig through the frozen ground and remove the coffin. There was no headstone on the grave, which made the disinterment simpler. The men carried the casket into the schoolhouse and placed it on the floor, then opened it and transferred the body onto two tables that had been pushed together for the autopsy.

Three physicians, Dr. George W. Knapp, Dr. Leancy Rupert and Dr. Lorenzo Houston McClung were chosen to perform the procedure, in order to ensure the results were accurate. Constable Shaver was present, and with him was Trout Shue, who had been 'encouraged' by the Constable to attend the examination. Justice Harlan McClung and a jury of five impartial men were also present, to verify the validity of the findings.

When the coffin was opened, the medical team was amazed that the body was still in such good condition. The below zero temperatures had kept the ground frozen, and Zona looked just as she did the day she was buried.

The doctors began their examination by checking the contents of the stomach for any trace of poison. None was found, but remarkably it showed that the last meal Zona ate included no trace of meat, only the fruits and preserves the ghost had told her mother about. Next, the doctors examined the uterus, which proved Zona had not been expecting a child; nor had she lost a child in the days before her death.

All during the examination, Trout repeatedly stated that Zona had died either of natural causes or of a fall down the stairs, and no crime had been committed. No one bothered to answer him, however, and the procedure continued.

As the doctors began to examine Zona's head, the room grew quiet. When they removed the stiff collar from Zona's dress, her head rolled to one side and finger shaped bruises on her slender neck were clearly visible.

On further investigation the physicians saw that her neck was dislocated between the first and second vertebrae, the ligaments were ruptured, and her windpipe had been crushed at the front of her neck (explaining the blood seen by Andy Jones when he first visited the house).

When one of the doctors stated that Zona had been murdered by strangulation, Trout Shoe leapt to his feet and shouted "They can't prove that *I* did it."

That evening, Zona's body was respectfully returned to the coffin and carried back to the graveyard, where it was placed into the ground and covered up. When Mary Heaster heard the results of the autopsy she gave thanks to God for answering her prayers and to Zona for appearing to her with the truth.

Greenbrier County Courthouse

Chapter Eight
The Trial

Immediately after the autopsy findings were released, Sheriff Hill Nickell arrested Trout Shue. A preliminary hearing was held, and enough evidence was presented to detain Trout in the Lewisburg jail, where he would await arraignment during the April term of the Circuit Court.

Trout did not seem to take his incarceration seriously, laughing and joking with his jailers and telling anyone who would listen that no one had ever been convicted on such flimsy circumstantial evidence. He said that even if Zona had been strangled, someone else could have killed her while he was working at the blacksmith shop.

The grand jury convened on Thursday,

April 22, 1897, at the Greenbrier County Courthouse; a stately brick structure which was built in 1837. The jury was presented with the facts of the case against Trout Shue. They all agreed there was enough evidence to indicate he may have caused the death of his wife Zona.

An indictment against Trout was drawn up, detailing the crime the defendant was accused of and declaring that E. S. Shue had pleaded not guilty of the charge. As a result of the indictment, Trout would be held in jail until the second day of the June term of the 1897 Greenbrier County Circuit Court, when he would stand trial for the murder of Zona Shue.

Trout, who had been sure that the charges against him would be dismissed by the grand jury, was extremely distressed when he learned that he was going to go to trial for Zona's murder and threatened to kill himself.

The jailers were told to keep a close watch and prevent his suicide if at all possible. Trout, however, soon recovered his arrogance, and set about compiling a list of some 120 character witnesses that he wanted his attorney to call on his behalf at court.

Trout Shue's trial was set to begin on June 23. Mary Heaster rented a room at the boarding house in Lewisburg so that she could be present each day, since she did not know when she would be called on to testify. Her husband Jacob stayed on the farm with the boys, caring for the crops and the livestock, which could not be left unattended.

Mary prayed each night that the Lord would let the jury find Trout guilty, for she knew in her heart that he had killed her darling Zona, her only daughter. She was confident that if the Lord had seen fit to send Zona to tell her about the murder, then He would surely meet out justice to Trout for what he had done.

Zona's mother patiently sat through the opening procedures of the trial. She could not recall when she had seen such a large crowd of people. Most of the activities taking place were meaningless to her, but she did take note of the judge and the jury.

The Honorable Judge Joseph Marcellus McWhorter was to hear the case. A jury of twelve men had already been chosen and were in place. Some of them knew the Heaster family, others did not. Most of the people in the county had already heard about the bizarre circumstances of the trial, as every newspaper in the area had been reporting on it since Trout's arrest. The names of the jurors were entered into the Law Order Book, and the stenographer Minnie Grose pledged under oath to take notes on the trial and transcribe them when she was asked to do so.

After what seemed like hours to Zona's mother, the trial got underway. Prosecuting Attorney Preston gave his opening remarks, telling the jurors that while the case itself was circumstantial, they were going to hear evidence "such has never been presented in any court before."

Mary was surprised to read an account of the opening day of the trial in the local newspaper the next day, since it was not usual for court cases in Greenbrier County to be so closely monitored. But, everyone agreed, this was not an ordinary case.

~~~~~~

Greenbrier Independent

June 24, 1897

Circuit Court convened on Tuesday, with Judge

J. M. McWhorter presiding. The case of the State vs. E. S. Shue, charged with the murder of his wife, was called yesterday afternoon. Both sides announced themselves ready and thereupon the following jury was sworn to try the case: A. B. Gardner, D. S. Lockhart, C. W. Dunbar, A. B. Stuart, C. W. Hogsett, J. M. Hughart, T. W. McClung, J. A. Vaughan, C. M. Thomasson, J. A. Hartsook, R. Blofield and J. R. Ridgway. The State's attorney, Mr. Preston, and Henry Gilmer, Esq., appear for the prosecution whilst the prisoner is defended by Dr. Rucker and Jamse P. D. Gardner. But little of the evidence had been heard when court adjourned yesterday afternoon.

~~~~~~

Over the next days, Preston called his witnesses to the stand, hoping to prove beyond a reasonable doubt that Shue had killed his wife. They included Dr. Knapp, Dr. Rupert, Dr. McClung, Martha Jones, her son Anderson and several others who had knowledge of the alleged crime.

Eventually, the prosecutor called out the name of Mrs. Mary Heaster, and a murmur went through the courtroom. Everyone assumed that she would be questioned about her daughter's ghost, but Preston only asked her about her dealings with Mr. Shue.

Mary was disappointed with his decision, but was not surprised; she understood that the lawyer did not want her to appear to be foolish or superstitious and thus taint the prosecution's case. So she was surprised when Trout's attorney brought up the very thing Preston had hoped to forgo. In a condescending tone, Dr. Rucker asked Mary a number of questions, to which she replied in a calm and reasonable way. The transcript from the trial was printed in the *Greenbrier Independent* Newspaper.

~~~~~~

Greenbrier Independent

July 1, 1897

MRS. MARY J. HEASTER, THE MOTHER OF MRS. SHUE, SEES HER DAUGHTER IN VISIONS

The following very remarkable testimony was given by Mrs. Heaster on the pending trial of E. S. Shue for the murder of his wife {her daughter}, and led to the inquest and post mortem examination, which resulted in Shue's arrest and trial. It was brought out by counsel for the accused:

Question. - I have heard that you had some dream or vision which led to this post mortem examination?

Answer. - They saw enough theirselves without me telling them. It was no dream - she came back and told me that he was mad that she didn't have no meat cooked for supper. But she said she had plenty, and said that she had butter and apple-butter, apples and named over two or three kinds of jellies, pears and cherries and raspberry jelly, and she says I had plenty; and she says don't you think that he was mad and just took down all my nice things and packed them away and just ruined them. And she told me where I could look down back of Aunt Martha Joneses, in the meadow, in a rocky place; that I could look in a cellar behind some loose planks and see. It was a square log house, and it was hewed up to the square, and she said for me to look right at the right-hand side of the door as you go in and at the right-hand corner as you go in. Well, I saw the place just exactly as she told me, and I saw blood right there where she told me; and she told me something about that meat every night she came, just as she did the first night. She came four times, and four nights; but the second night she told me that her neck was squeezed off at the first joint and it was just as she told me.

Q.- Now, Mrs. Heaster, this sad affair was very particularly impressed upon your mind, and there was not a moment during your waking hours that you did not dwell upon it?

A. - No, sir; and there is not yet, either.

Q. - And was this not a dream founded upon your distressed condition of mind?

A. - No, sir. It was no dream, for I was as wide awake as I ever was.

Q. - Then if not a dream or dreams, what do you call it?

A. - I prayed to the Lord that she might come

back and tell me what had happened; and I
prayed that she might come herself and tell on
him.

Q. - Do you think that you actually saw her in
flesh and blood?

A. - Yes, sir, I do. I told them the very dress
that she was killed in, and when she went to
leave me she turned her head completely around
and looked at me like she wanted me to know
all about it. And the very next time she came
back to me she told me all about it. The first
time she came, she seemed that she did not want
to tell me as much about it as she did afterwards.
The last night she was there she told me that she
did everything she could do, and I am satisfied
that she did do all that, too.

Q. - Now, Mrs. Heaster, don't you know that
these visions, as you term them or describe
them, were nothing more or less than four

dreams founded upon your distress?

A. - No, I don't know it. The Lord sent her to me to tell it. I was the only friend that she knew she could tell and put any confidence in; I was the nearest one to her. He gave me a ring that he pretended she wanted me to have; but I don't know what dead woman he might have taken it off of. I wanted her own ring and he would not let me have it.

Q. - Mrs. Heaster, are you positively sure that these are not four dreams?

A. - Yes, sir. It was not a dream. I don't dream when I am wide awake, to be sure; and I know I saw her right there with me.

Q. - Are you not considerably superstitious?

A. - No, sir, I'm not. I was never that way before, and am not now.

Q. - Do you believe the scriptures?

A. - Yes, sir. I have no reason not to believe it.

Q. - And do you believe the scriptures contain the words of God and his Son?

A. - Yes, sir, I do. Don't you believe it?

Q. - Now, I would like if I could, to get you to say that these were four dreams and not four visions or appearances of your daughter in flesh and blood?

A. - I am not going to say that; for I am not going to lie.

Q. - Then you insist that she actually appeared in flesh and blood to you upon four different occasions?

A. - Yes, sir.

Q. - Did she not have any other conversation with you other than upon the matter of her death?

A. - Yes, sir, some other little things. Some things I have forgotten - just a few words. I just wanted the particulars about her death, and I got

73

them.

Q. - When she came did you touch her?

A. - Yes, sir. I got up on my elbows and reached out a little further, as I wanted to see if people came in their coffins, and I sat up and leaned on my elbow and there was light in the house. It was not a lamp light. I wanted to see if there was a coffin, but there was not. She was just like she was when she left this world. It was just after I went to bed, and I wanted her to come and talk to me, and she did. This was before the inquest and I told my neighbors. They said she was exactly as I told them she was.

Q. - Had you ever seen the premises where your daughter lived?

A. - No, sir, I had not; but I found them just exactly as she told me it was, and I never laid eyes on that house until since her death. She told me this before I knew anything of the buildings at all.

Q. - How long was it after this when you had these interviews with your daughter until you did see buildings?

A. - It was a month or more after the examination. It has been a little over a month since I saw her.

RE-CROSS EXAMINATION.

Q. - You said your daughter told you that down by the fence in a rocky place you would find some things?

A. - She said for me to look there. She didn't say I would find some things, but for me to look there.

Q. - Did she tell you what to look for?

A. - No, she did not. I was so glad to see her I forgot to ask her.

Q. - Have you ever examined that place since?

A. - Yes, sir. We looked at the fence a little but didn't find anything.

~~~~~~

Mary also told the defense attorney about the sheet she had taken from Zona's coffin, and how it had turned the water pink, like blood, when she washed it. When she finished her testimony, Mary felt she had finally allowed Zona to reveal what had happened to her.

Neither the prosecutor nor the defense lawyer objected to the testimony, so the judge did not declare it inadmissable. It was the only time the testimony of a ghost was accepted into a court record in a United States murder trial.

On the sixth day, Trout took the stand in his own defense. The *Greenbrier Independent* paper reported his testimony.

~~~~~~

Greenbrier Independent

July 1, 1897

THE STATE VERSUS E.S. SHUE

The evidence in this case was concluded
yesterday morning and the argument begun in
the afternoon, after the instructions had been
given to the jury by the Court. There was no
witness to the crime charged against Shue and
the State rests its case for a conviction wholly
on the circumstances connecting the accused
with the murder charged. The evidence of the
medical experts, Dr. Knapp and others, who
conducted the post mortem examination, makes
it quite clear that Mrs. Shue did not commit
suicide. The post mortem made it clear that her
neck had been dislocated, but there was no mark
upon her person or other evidence to show that
she had subjected herself to any sort of violence.
Her body was found by the negro boy, sent to

the house by Shue, about 11 o'clock in the morning, and when Dr. Knapp reached the house, an hour or two later, it was quite cold and he was satisfied that she was then dead, though he resorted, without effect, to various means of resuscitation. We mention the following, among other circumstances relied upon by the State to show that Shue killed his wife by dislocating her neck by some means the evidence does not disclose; that he was the only person seen about or known to have been at the house that morning prior to the time when his wife was found dead; that he requested Dr. Knapp, after he had resorted to the usual means of resuscitation, to make no further examination of the body; that he assisted in dressing the body and in doing so put around the neck a high collar and a large veil several times folded and tied in a large bow under the chin; that the head was observed by a number of the witnesses to be very loose upon the neck and would drop from side to side when not supported; that Shue sent the negro boy to the house to gather the eggs, instructing him to go into the house, find his wife and see if she wanted anything; that in his conversation and conduct, after his wife's death, he seemed in good spirits, and showed no proper appreciation of the loss he had sustained; that when summoned to the inquest and post mortem out at Sewell he said to various witnesses that he knew he would come back under arrest; that in speaking to a number of witnesses on the subject he always said he knew that they could not prove that he did the killing. So the connection of the accused with the crime depends entirely upon the strength of the circumstantial evidence introduced by the State. Shue was on the stand all Tuesday afternoon.

He was given free rein and talked at great length; was very minute and particular in describing unimportant incidents; denied pretty much everything said by other witnesses; said the prosecution was all spite work; entered a positive denial of the charge against him; vehemently protested his innocence, calling God to witness; admitted that he had served a term in the pen; declared that he dearly loved his wife, and appealed to the jury to look into his face and then say if he was guilty. His testimony, manner, and so forth, made an unfavorable impression on the spectators. There is no middle ground for the jury to take. The verdict inevitably and logically, must be for murder in the first degree or for an acquittal.

~~~~~~

On the last day of June, the prosecution and defense gave their final arguments and the jury was sequestered so they could make a decision as to whether Trout Shue was guilty of murder. It took only an hour for them to do so.

Trout stood and listened as the verdict was read : "We the jury find Erasmus S. {alias E.S.} Shue guilty of murder in the first degree as charged in the within indictment, and we further find that he be punished by confinement in the penitentiary." Trout narrowly escaped being hanged, as ten of the jurors had voted for him to be executed.

When Mary heard the verdict, she quietly gave thanks to God, and to her daughter Zona, who had come back from her grave to make sure that justice was done. For the first time since her death, Mary believed that Zona was at peace.

The *Greenbrier Independent* covered the trial until the jury reached a verdict.

Greenbrier Independent

July 8, 1897

SHUE CONVICTED OF MURDER

After an elaborate argument of the evidence by
Messrs. Gilmer and Preston for the State and
Jas. P. D. Gardner, colored, and Dr. Rucker for
the accused, the case of the State vs. E. S.
("Trout") Shue was given to the jury last
Thursday afternoon, and the jury, after being out
one hour and ten minutes, returned into Court
with a verdict of murder in the first degree, as
charged in the indictment, but recommending
that the accused be punished by imprisonment,
which means, under the law, that he be confined
in the penitentiary for the term of his natural
life. Dr. Rucker entered a motion for a new
trial, but this was withdrawn the next morning,
and Shue will be duly sentenced before the

Court adjourns. Though the evidence was entirely circumstantial, the verdict meets general approval, as all who heard the evidence are satisfied of the prisoner's guilt. After the murder Shue had every opportunity to make his escape, as four weeks elapsed before he was arrested and put in jail. The fact that he did not do so was explained by Mr. Gilmer, in his argument, by showing that Shue was all the time laboring under the impression that he could not be convicted on circumstantial evidence, and felt secure in knowing that there was no witness but himself, to the crime. This, Mr. Gilmer argued, showed not a lack of sense, but information, and accounts for Shue's presence at the inquest and his oft repeated remark that they could not show he did it. Taking the verdict of the jury as ascertaining the truth, then we must conclude that Shue deliberately broke his wife's neck -

probably with his strong hands - and with no other motive than to be rid of her that he might get another more to his liking. And, if so, his crime is one of the most horrible, cruel and revolting ever known in the history of this county. Mr. Preston deserves the thanks of the people for his diligence in hunting up the evidence and for his admirable management of the case before the jury.

The *Monroe Watchman*, a prominent newspaper from nearby Monroe County, sent one of their reporters to witness the trial and write an account of the proceedings. His findings were reported in the paper.

The Monroe Watchman

July 1, 1897

About 10 o'clock on the morning of the day,

January 23, 1897, on which Mrs. E. S. Shue was found dead, E. S. Shue, the prisoner, after having been to his black-smith shop, went to the house of a negro woman and asked the son of this woman to go to his house and hunt the eggs and then to go to Mrs. Shue and see if she wanted to send to the store for anything. This negro boy went to the house of Shue, and after looking for the eggs and finding none, he went to the house, knocked and receiving no response, opened the door and went in. He found the dead body of Mrs. Shue lying upon the floor. The body was lying stretched out perfectly straight with feet together, one hand lying by the side and the other lying across the body, the head was slightly inclined to one side. The negro boy ran and told his mother that Mrs. Shue was dead and then went on to the black-smith shop and told E. S. Shue, the prisoner, that his wife was dead. Shue and the negro woman ran to the house, both arriving there at about the same time. Dr. Knapp was called in after the body had been laid out and dressed, and pronounced Mrs. Shue dead. The dress in which the corpse was dressed had a high stiff collar. There were slight discolorations on the right side of the neck and the right cheek. The Doctor unfastened the collar and examined the front of the neck and was about to examine the back of the neck when Shue, the .... that he desisted from further examination and left the house. The body was taken to the Meadows and buried. A few weeks afterward owing to the suspicious conduct and conversations of the prisoner, a post mortem examination was ordered. This examination was conducted by Drs. Knapp, Rupert and McClung. The examination disclosed that the neck was dislocated between the first and second cerebral vertebrae. The ligaments were torn and ruptured. The wind-pipe had been crushed in at a point in front of the neck. All other portions and organs of the body were apparently in a perfectly healthy state. The defense had finished most of its evidence Tuesday evening but had proved little to show the innocence of the prisoner. The prisoner's statement amounted, for the most part, to a denial in detail of the State's evidence.

~~~~~~

The Pocahontas Times, a newspaper in Trout Shue's hometown carried an unflattering article about him shortly after the trial, making it clear that the residents of Droop Mountain felt only relief that the prisoner had been found guilty of the crime. Neither was any protest from Trout's parents, Jacob Thomas and

Elizabeth Shue, ever voiced in any public place or in any of the other numerous newspapers that were closely following the story.

~~~~~~

The Pocahontas Times

July 9, 1897

Trout Shue, formerly of Droop Mountain, was found guilty of murder in the first degree, in the Greenbrier County Court, with the jury recommending a life sentence. The evidence was convincing that Shue had murdered his wife by breaking her neck, and the case presented this aspect, that the woman died of a broken neck, and that it was impossible for her to break it herself, and that no one could have done it except her husband. What was the closing scene of the woman's life will probably never be known, but the explanation of the 'vision' of the woman's mother gives a very striking suggestion of the last quarrel which ended in the death of the woman. She said that her daughter appeared to her and said on the last evening she had gotten a good supper except there was no meat on the table, and that her husband had become enraged on account of it. Shue is a bad man and he has no sympathy from the neighborhood in which he was raised.

West Virginia State Penitentiary

Chapter Nine
Moundsville Prison

After the sentencing, Trout Shue was housed in the Lewisburg jail, pending his transportation to Moundsville Prison. Many of the local townspeople felt that because of the heinous murder he had committed, Trout should have been sentenced to hang, which was legal in the state of West Virginia. Numerous citizens of Greenbrier County voiced their anger to a well known reporter at *The Greenbrier Independent* newspaper, which published the following article a few days later.

~~~~~~

The Greenbrier Independent

July 15, 1897

"Ever since the termination of the trial of E. S. Shue for the murder of his wife and his conviction for murder in the first degree with a recommendation by the jury that his punishment should be imprisonment, there have been whisperings and rumors that mob violence might be a possibility..."

~~~~~~

As more stories were circulated about Trout, and as word of his mistreatment and abandonment of his first wife and the possible murder of his second wife became known, many of the men in Greenbrier County became convinced that he deserved to be lynched, not sent to prison. Rumors began to spread that Trout was to be forcibly taken from the jail on Washington Street in Lewisburg and be summarily hung.

A group of more than thirty angry men gathered at the Brushy Ridge campground, which was located on the west side of the county seat. They made plans to kidnap Shue from the jail and hang him. The men were heavily armed and extremely agitated.

Several farmers who lived near the campground overheard the men talking about taking Shue by force from the jail. Fearing that many people could be hurt or killed in an attempt to kidnap Trout, some of the men traveled to the home of Sheriff Nickell, who lived at Meadow Bluff. After listening to their report, the Sheriff thanked the men for alerting him, and headed for Lewisburg.

About the same time, Deputy Sheriff Dwyer, who was standing guard duty at the jail, learned of the plot from another group of men who had been fishing at Brushy Ridge. Trout overheard their conversation about the planned lynching. He began to tremble so badly that he could not dress himself, and asked for a priest so that he could make a confession.

After helping Trout with his attire, Deputy Sheriff Dwyer handcuffed him, and at sundown the two men mounted horses and rode until they came to a cornfield a few miles outside of Lewisburg. Dwyer hollowed out an opening in one of the corn shocks in the field, and secreted Trout inside it. He then kept watch nearby for any sign of the lynch party.

Meanwhile, Sheriff Nickell managed to head off the mob near the campground. The Sheriff was able to reason with them, and sent everyone home.

Shue was returned to the jailhouse just before dawn, exhausted but unharmed. The next day bench warrants were issued for the leaders of the lynch party, including C. Martin, J. Nary, Robert Hunter and Otey Arbaugh.

Considering the circumstances, town

officials felt that it would be best to remand Trout Shue to the Moundsville State Penitentiary as soon as possible. Sheriff Nickell left Lewisburg with the prisoner on July 13, 1897.

The two men arrived at the prison on July 14, and Trout was taken into custody. He was assigned prison number 3255, and was described on his prison file card as being 35 years old and having most recently lived in Greenbrier County. His occupation was entered on the card as blacksmith (which would again be his job at the prison) and his personal description stated that he had blue eyes and dark brown hair.

The file also recorded that Shue had numerous scars on his body, including one on his stomach, one above each ear, one on his shin and four on the back of his head. It was obvious that he had been involved in several serious altercations since his last stay at the penitentiary.

From all accounts, Shue was a broken man during his second incarceration at the state prison. No one, including any members of the Shue family, were ever recorded as having come to visit him.

Shue had always enjoyed drawing, and whenever he could find a bit of paper and a pencil, he would spend hours in his cell making intricate and fanciful pictures. Trout's most famous work of art depicted Zona and himself beneath a tree at the bottom of a picture, while at the same time they could be seen lying in their coffins at the top of the picture. For some unknown reason, Trout asked one of the guards to mail the picture to Charlie Tuckwiller, who owned the blacksmith shop in Livesay's Mill where Trout had been employed when he met Zona Heaster.

The drawing may have been Trout's way of coming to terms with what he had done to his wife. Or perhaps Zona had begun visiting his bedside at night in the prison, with her head turned all the way around. Trout may have hoped her spirit would follow the picture wherever it went, and leave him in peace.

Whitegate Cemetery

Chapter Ten
Trout's Death

In the early spring of 1900, an epidemic of influenza swept through the West Virginia countryside. Dozens of prisoners who were incarcerated at the state prison died from the virus.

Trout Shue, who was in the third year of his life sentence, contracted the illness. Even though he was not yet forty, and in good physical health, his body deteriorated quickly.

When he realized he was not going to recover, Trout wrote a letter to his mother, reporting to her that he was dying and asking her not to worry about him. He told her that he loved her, and promised that someday they would meet again in Heaven.

Trout Shue died in the West Virginia

Sate Prison on March 13, 1900. No one from the Shue family came to claim his body, so he was buried in the Whitegate Cemetery, which was created by an act of the West Virginia Legislature in 1897.

The cemetery was built along Tom's Run, about a half a mile from the main route into Moundsville. It was the final resting place for prisoners whose bodies were unclaimed when they died in the State Penitentiary.

Although the prison originally placed wooden markers on the graves, Tom's Creek flooded in 1927, and many of the markers were washed away. Consequently, after the flood there was nothing left to show the exact location where Trout Shue's body was buried in the cemetery.

Epilogue

Zona's mother, Mary Jane Heaster, lived for almost twenty years after Trout Shue's trial. During that time, many people believed that Zona literally came back from the grave to reveal that she was murdered to her mother. Others thought that originally Mary only had suspicions that Trout had killed Zona, and had made up the dream in order to have her death investigated. Later, they said, Mary added more details to the story after Zona's strangulation was revealed in the autopsy.

Mary Heaster was known as an honest, God fearing woman to everyone in her community. She always maintained that her testimony at the trial was true, and that she had shared the details of Zona's ghostly visit with a number of her friends and neighbors *before* the autopsy took place.

Below is a copy of a letter that Mary Heaster wrote in answer to an inquiry she received from The American Society for Psychical Research (ASPR). The ASPR was founded in 1885 by a distinguished group of scholars and scientists, and is the oldest Psychical research organization in the US. Many of the early members were pioneers in psychology, psychiatry, physics and astronomy. They studied ESP, telepathy, hypnosis, and the possibility of life after death.

Mary's ghostly encounter was of great interest to the ASPR. Her letters to them were printed in *The Journal of the American Society for Psychical Research*. Today, the letters are Mary's own testimony to us from beyond the grave, if you will, ensuring us that Zona's ghost did return to reveal she was murdered.

Little Sewell Mt. W.Va.

August 3, 1897

Richard Hodgson, Esq.

Boston, Mass.

Dear Sir:

Your letter of recent date at hand as was sent me by Mr. Gilmer. My vision about the murder of my daughter by her husband E. Shue, is as follows. My daughter was found dead where they lived near Livesay's Mill, by a colored boy Jan 23, 1897; was brought to my house Jan. 24.

I was not satisfied in regard to her death. I incessantly prayed the Lord to send her back to tell me all about her death. She came back four times and told me; "He was mad. I had no meat cooked, but I had butter, apple butter, apples, preserved pears, cherries and three kinds of jellies and plenty on the

103

table." She said "It is the last joint and squeezed til it was all bloody" (but I did not know what she meant until the body was taken up and found that it was the last joint of the neck that was dislocated and bloody).

She told me to look at the house, to go in through the house to the log building and to look at the right side as I went in the door. (This we did and we found there had been a scuffle or sign of the same and also blood on the floor.)

She said too to look in the cellar behind some loose plank and also to go down next to Martha Joneses' in the hollow and look at a rocky place near the fence. This we did and found nothing. She told me he has taken my clothes all down and taken them away and had taken my pictures and pretties down from the walls and put them in a basket where there had been some wool and all spoilt them. *(By examination we found this to be a fact.)* She said further that she had done everything she could do. I had a hold of her arm and she appeared natural. I got up in the bed and felt over the same to see if her coffin was there and it was not.

As she started away she said she had to walk and go by herself away around and then she turned her head squarely around and put her bonnet in under her arm and continued looking at me until she disappeared at the door. She had on the same clothes that the women say she had on when he dressed her. There was a fire light in the house. I was wide awake.

This page is rather explanatory. I have aimed to enclose my explanation in parenthesis so you would understand it all better. If you do

not understand any part of it let me know and I
will make it all as plain as I can. It is stated in
such a disconnected way that it is not as plain
to the reader as it was to the one that had the
conversation and realized what they were
talking about.

> *Very Truly Yours,*
> *Mary J. Heaster*

Mary Heaster wrote a second letter to the researcher about a month later, sending him the names and addresses of persons who were witnesses to the fact that she had told them before the autopsy that Zona was murdered by having her throat crushed.

> *Little Sewell Mt., W.Va.*
> *Sept. 6, 1897*

Dear Sir,

In reply to your letter of Aug. 21, I give

you the following names of persons to whom I had related my vision before I knew anything of the facts in regard to the death of my daughter: Miss Catherine Bivens; Little Sewell Mt., W.Va.; Miss Allie B. Jones, Little Sewell Mt., W.Va.; Mr. C. G. Martin, Little Sewell Mt., W.Va.; Mr. L. E. Heaster, Little Sewell Mt., W.Va.; Mr. J. H. Heaster, Little Sewell Mt., W.Va.; Mr. A. N. Heaster, Maywood, Fayette Co., W.Va.; Miss Candice Eagle, Meadow Bluff, W.Va.

Mr. Gilmer is acquainted with the facts, for he was assistant prosecuting attorney in the case. I have never had any experience of a similar nature either before or since the times I wrote to you.

Very truly yours,

M. J. Heaster

All of those named sent letters stating

that Mary Heaster told them about the ghostly visit and how Zona said she had died from a broken neck before the autopsy took place.

DOCUMENTATION

Greenbrier Ghost Historical Marker

Source

http://www.wvculture.org/history/markers/markerinfo.html

The West Virginia Highway Historical Marker Program was initiated in 1937 as part of the New Deal as a way to encourage tourism during the Great Depression. The West Virginia Historic Commission took over the program in 1963. According to the program guidelines, the site, property, district, or community honored with a marker must possess some degree of significance in state or local prehistory (archaeology), history, natural history, architecture, or cultural life.

The Greenbrier Ghost Historical Marker was erected in 1979, and is located on Highway 60, just off the I-64 exit 156, southwest side.

GREENBRIER GHOST

Interred in nearby cemetery is Zona Heaster Shue. Her death in 1897 was presumed natural until her spirit appeared to her mother to describe how she was killed by her husband Edward. Autopsy on the exhumed body verified the apparition's account. Edward, found guilty of murder, was sentenced to the state prison. Only known case in which testimony from ghost helped convict a murderer.

WEST VIRGINIA DEPARTMENT OF CULTURE AND HISTORY 1981

Zona Heaster Shue Gravestone

Source

http://www.umc.org/find-a-church/church/24322

Zona Heaster Shue is buried in the cemetery of the Soule Chapel United Methodist Church, which is located on Soule Chapel Lane near Farmdale Road in Meadow Bluff, West Virginia. Her grave had no headstone until 1979, when members of the church raised the money to provide one.

Drawing by Trout Shue

Source

http://www.greenbrierhistorical.org/the-north-house-museum.html

Trout Shue made a drawing of himself and Zona Heaster Shue while he was a prisoner in the West Virginia State Penitentiary. He mailed the picture to his former employer, Charlie Tuckwiller of Livesay's Mill. The original drawing is currently displayed by the Greenbrier Historical Society at the North House Museum in Lewisburg, West Virginia.

Zona Heaster in the 1800 Federal Census

Source

Year: 1880; Census Place: Meadow Bluff, Greenbrier, West
Virginia; Roll: 1402; Page: 342C; Enumeration District: 035
Original data: Tenth Census of the United States, 1880. (NARA
microfilm publication T9, 1,454 rolls). Records of the Bureau of the
Census, Record Group 29. National Archives, Washington, D.C.

Elva J. Heaster
in the 1880 United States Federal Census

Name:	Elva J. Heaster
	[Alva Z Heaster]
	[Elva Zona Heaster]
Age:	7
Birth Date:	Abt 1873
Birthplace:	West Virginia
Home in 1880:	Meadow Bluff, Greenbrier, West Virginia, USA
Dwelling Number:	190
Race:	White
Gender:	Female
Relation to Head of House:	Daughter
Marital status:	Single
Father's name:	Jacob H. Heaster
Father's Birthplace:	Virginia
Mother's name:	Mary J. Heaster
Mother's Birthplace:	Virginia
Occupation:	At School
Attended School:	Yes
Cannot Read:	Yes
Cannot Write:	Yes
Neighbors:	View others on page

Household Members:

Name	Age
Jacob H. Heaster	32
Mary J. Heaster	30
Alfred N. Heaster	8
Elva J. Heaster	7
John M. Heaster	6
Lewis E. Heaster	3/12

117

Baby Woldridge Birth Record
Child of Zona Heaster

Source

Ancestry.com. West Virginia, Births Index, 1804-1938 [database on-line]. From digital images of copies of originals housed in County Courthouses throughout West Virginia. Birth records. This database contains an index extracted from microfilmed copies of various West Virginia birth records.

The birth record of Zona Heaster's infant can also be reasonably taken as a death record, since no first name was given to the baby. This was common in cases where a newborn child only lived a short time.

To view the original document go to:

http://www.wvculture.org/vrr/va_view.aspx?Id=49963

2&Type=Birth (Record # 310)

118

Woldridge

in the West Virginia, Births Index, 1804-1938

Name: Woldridge

Gender: Male

Race: White

Birth Date: 29 Nov 1895

Birth Place: Little Sewell Mtn., Greenbrier, West Virginia

Father: George Woldridge

Mother: Zona Heaster

FHL Film Number: 595033

Zona Heaster/Trout Shue Marriage

Source

Ancestry.com. West Virginia, Marriages Index, 1785-1971
[database on-line]. Ancestry.com Operations, Inc., 2011.
"West Virginia Marriages, 1853–1970." Index. Digital images of
originals housed in County Courthouses in various counties
throughout West Virginia. Beginning in 1853 Virginia law (which
still applied to counties that would make up West Virginia) required
counties to issue marriage licenses and record marriages in registers.
Prior to this, Virginia law required that church marriages be
recorded in registers, and starting in 1780, copies of these registers
had to be forwarded to civil authorities. Details contained in this
index were extracted from these county marriage records, which
include bonds, applications, licenses, register entries, and returns.

To view the original document go to:

http://www.wvculture.org/vrr/va_view.aspx?Id=10980

570&Type=Marriage (Line 126).

E Z Heaster
in the West Virginia, Marriages Index, 1785-1971

Name: E Z Heaster

Gender: Female

Birth Date: abt 1874

Birth Place: Greenbrier County, West Virginia

Age: 22

Spouse's name: E S Shue

Spouse Gender: Male

Spouse Age: 29

Spouse Birth Place: Augusta

Marriage Date: 20 Oct 1896

Marriage Place: Greenbrier County, West Virginia

Zona Heaster Shue Death Record

Source

Ancestry.com. West Virginia, Deaths Index, 1853-1973 - database "West Virginia Deaths, 1853–1970." Index. From originals housed in county courthouses throughout West Virginia. "Death Records.". West Virginia counties began recording deaths in 1853, in accordance with Virginia state laws. Statewide registration of deaths began in 1917. Compliance with the 1917 law—and, thus, the percentage of deaths registered—increased over time. Initially, deaths were recorded in register books; later, certificates were submitted to the state. This database is an index extracted from microfilmed copies of county death records. The FHL film number refers to a microfilm copy of the source held by the Family History Library in Salt Lake City, Utah.

To view the original document go to :

http://www.wvculture.org/vrr/va_view.aspx?Id=28980 07&Type=Death (# 59).

E Zona Shue

in the West Virginia, Deaths Index, 1853-1973

Name: E. Zona Shue

Birth Date: abt 1875

Birth Place: Greenbrier Co

Death Date: 23 Jan 1897

Death Place: Livesays Mill, Greenbrier, West Virginia

Burial Date: 25 Jan 1897

Physician: Dr. George W. Knapp

Cause of Death:: Child birth

Marital status: Married

Gender: Female

HL Film Number: 595030

Trout Shue in the1870 Federal Census

Source

Year: 1870; Census Place: District 3, Augusta, Virginia; Roll: M593_1634; Page: 367A; Family History Library Film: 553133

Ancestry.com. 1870 United States Federal Census [database on-line]. Ancestry.com Operations, Inc., 2009. 1870 U.S. census, population schedules. NARA microfilm publication M593, 1,761 rolls. Washington, D.C.: National Archives and Records Administration, n.d.

Stirbling T Shue
in the 1870 United States Federal Census

Name:	Stirbling T Shue
	[Stribling T Shue]
Age in 1870:	8
Birth Year:	abt 1862
Birthplace:	Virginia
Dwelling Number:	253
Home in 1870:	District 3, Augusta, Virginia
Race:	White
Gender:	Male
Inferred Father:	Jacob T Shue
Inferred Mother:	Elizabeth Shue

Household Members:

Name	Age
Jacob T Shue	39
Elizabeth Shue	34
Susan V Shue	14
James W Shue	13
Joseph W Shue	11
Stirbling T Shue	8
Fannie Lee Shue	5
John P Shue	3
Maggie A Shue	2

Ellen (Allie) Cutlip Marriage Record

Source

Ancestry.com. West Virginia, Marriages Index, 1785-1971 [database on-line]. Ancestry.com Operations, Inc., 2011.Original data: "West Virginia Marriages, 1853–1970." Index. FamilySearch, Salt Lake City, Utah, 2008, 2009. Digital images of originals housed in County Courthouses in various counties throughout West Virginia. Beginning in 1853 Virginia law (which still applied to counties that would make up West Virginia) required counties to issue marriage licenses and record marriages in registers. Prior to this, Virginia law required that church marriages be recorded in registers, and starting in 1780, copies of these registers had to be forwarded to civil authorities. Details contained in this index were extracted from these county marriage records, which include bonds, applications, licenses, register entries, and returns.

To view the original document go to: http://www.wvculture.org/vrr/va_view.aspx?Id=10979 846&Type=Marriage (#202).

Ellen E Cutlip
West Virginia, Marriages Index, 1785-1971

Name:	Ellen E Cutlip
Gender:	Female
Birth Date:	abt 1863
Birth Place:	Greenbrier County, West Virginia
Age:	22
Spouse's name:	E S Skue
Spouse Gender:	Male
Spouse Age:	24
Spouse Birth Place:	Augusta County
Marriage Date:	24 Dec 1885
Marriage Place:	Greenbrier, West Virginia

Girta L Shue in the 1900 Federal Census

Source

Year: 1900; Census Place: Falling Spring, Greenbrier, West Virginia; Page: 8; Enumeration District: 0028; FHL microfilm: 1241759 Source Information: Ancestry.com. 1900 United States Federal Census [database on-line]: Operations Inc, 2004. Original data: United States of America, Bureau of the Census. Twelfth Census of the United States, 1900. Washington, D.C.: National Archives and Records Administration, 1900. T623, 1854 rolls.This database is an index to all individuals enumerated in the 1900 United States Federal Census, the Twelfth Census of the United States. In addition, the names of those listed on the population schedule are linked to actual images of the 1900 Federal Census, copied from the National Archives and Records Administration microfilm, T623, 1854 rolls.

Girtie L Shue
in the 1900 United States Federal Census

Name:	Girtie L Shue
Age:	13
Birth Date:	Feb 1887
Birthplace:	West Virginia
Home in 1900:	Falling Spring, Greenbrier, West Virginia
Sheet Number:	8
Number of Dwelling in Order of Visitation:	122
Family Number:	122
Race:	White
Gender:	Female
Relation to Head of House:	Granddaughter
Marital status:	Single
Father's Birthplace:	Virginia
Mother's Birthplace:	West Virginia
Attended School:	6
Can Read:	Yes
Can Write:	Yes
Can Speak English:	Yes

Household Members:

Name	Age
Tinker A Mc Millian	25
Alie E Mc Millian	32
Clarance F Mc Millian	2
James R Mc Millian	1
Girtie L Shue	13

Trout Shue/ Lucy Tritt Marriage Record

Source

Ancestry.com. West Virginia, Marriages Index, 1785-1971
[database on-line]: Ancestry.com Operations, Inc., 2011.
"West Virginia Marriages, 1853–1970." Index. Digital images of
originals housed in County Courthouses in various counties
throughout West Virginia. Marriage records. Beginning in 1853
Virginia law (which still applied to counties that would make up
West Virginia) required counties to issue marriage licenses and
record marriages in registers. Prior to this, Virginia law required
that church marriages be recorded in registers, and starting in 1780,
copies of these registers had to be forwarded to civil authorities.
Details contained in this index were extracted from these county
marriage records, which include bonds, applications, licenses,
register entries, and returns.

Erasmus E Shoe
West Virginia, Marriages Index, 1785-1971

Name:	Erasmus E Shoe
	[*Erasmus E Shue*]
	[*Trout Shue*]
Gender:	Male
Birth Date:	abt 1862
Birth Place:	Augusta County, Virginia
Age:	32
Spouse's name:	Lucy A Tritt
Spouse Gender:	Female
Spouse Age:	24
Spouse Birth Place:	Greenbrier County, West Virginia
Marriage Date:	23 Jun 1894
Marriage Place:	Greenbrier County, West Virginia

Trout Shue Death Record

Source

https://www.findagrave.com/memorial/40813714/

erasmus-stribbling-shue

Trout Shue died on March 13, 1900, according to the records of the Moundsville Penitentiary. No one claimed his body, so he was buried in the Whitegate Cemetery. The *Wheeling Intelligencer* Newspaper - May 2, 1992 states: "Whitegate Cemetery is located along Tom's Run, about 3/4 of a mile from the main route into Moundsville on Fourth Street. It is probably more than 100 years old and is the final resting place for prisoners, unclaimed by anyone, from the former West Virginia Penitentiary in Moundsville."

Erasmus Stribbling "Edward" Trout Shue

in the U.S., Find A Grave Index, 1600s-Current

BIRTH	1861
	Mount Solon, Augusta County, Virginia, USA
DEATH	13 Mar 1900 (aged 38–39)
	Moundsville, Marshall County, West Virginia, USA
BURIAL	White Gate Cemetery
	Moundsville, Marshall County, West Virginia, USA
MEMORIAL ID	40813714 · View Source

The wife of Edward Shue is known as The Greenbrier Ghost, her death in 1897 was presumed natural until her spirit appeared to her mother to describe how she was killed by her husband Edward. Autopsy on the exhumed body verified the apparition's account. Edward, found guilty of murder, was sentenced to the state prison. Only known case in which testimony from a ghost helped convict a murderer.

Mary Robinson/Jacob Heaster Marriage

Source

Ancestry.com. West Virginia, Marriages Index, 1785-1971 [database on-line]. Provo, UT, USA: Ancestry.com Operations, Inc., 2011. "West Virginia Marriages, 1853–1970." Index. FamilySearch, Salt Lake City, Utah, 2008, 2009. Digital images of originals housed in County Courthouses in various counties throughout West Virginia. Marriage records.

Mary Jane Robinson

in the West Virginia, Marriages Index, 1785-1971

Name: Mary Jane Robinson

Gender: Female

Birth Date: abt 1850

Birth Place: Greenbrier County, West Virginia

Age: 20

Spouse's name: Jacob H Easther

Spouse Gender: Male

Spouse Age: 22

Spouse Birth Place: Greenbrier, West Virginia

Marriage Date: 3 Nov 1870

Marriage Place: Greenbrier, West Virginia

Marital status: Single

Father's name: Jno Robinson

Mother's name: Jemima Robinson

Spouse Father's Name: Jas Easther

Spouse Mother's Name: Margaret Easther

Mary Jane Heaster Death Record

Source

https://www.findagrave.com/memorial/77549777/

mary-jane-heaster

Ancestry.com. U.S., Find A Grave Index, 1600s-Current [database on-line]: Ancestry.com Operations, Inc., 2012. Original data: Find A Grave. Find A Grave. http://www.findagrave.com/cgi-bin/fg.cgi

Mary Jane Heaster

Find A Grave Index for Burials

Name: Mary Jane Heaster

Maiden Name: Robinson

Gender: Female

Birth Date: 15 Dec 1849

Birth Place: Greenbrier County, West Virginia

Death Date: 6 Sep 1916

Death Place: Greenbrier County, West Virginia

Baltimore Maryland Newspaper Article

Source

The Baltimore American Newspaper

Baltimore, M.D.

July 5, 1897

Mother-In-law's Vision as Evidence.

Ronceverte, W. Va., July 2.—Some time ago the wife of E. S. Shue was found dead in her home. A coroner's jury rendered a verdict, "death by heart disease." Neighbors were not satisfied, the woman's body was exhumed, and her neck was found broken. Shue was indicted, convicted and sentenced to the penitentiary for life. The principal evidence was that of Shue's mother-in-law, who testified that her daughter's spirit had come to her at a seance and said Shue had killed her by breaking her neck. All the other evidence was purely circumstantial.

Beckley West Virginia Newspaper Article

Source

Post-Herald and Register Beckley, West Virginia

November 12, 1977

Shirley Donnelly

Shirley Donnelly was an author and newspaper journalist. He was also the President of the West Virginia Historical Society and an ordained minister. Donnelly wrote many articles on the Greenbrier Ghost, and spoke with hundreds of people that were involved with the story.

Much of Donnelly's information came from Reuben Jones, who was the brother of Andy Jones (who found the body of Zona Heaster Shue). Reuben identified several early photographs of the couple as being authentic for Donnelly, including their wedding photo.

Ghost Solved Crime

By SHIRLEY DONNELLY

There's an area ghost story that will not down a bit more than that of Banquo's ghost.

It is the oft told tale that was but recently printed in a Charleston publication known as "The Moonlighter," the brain child of a brace of fellows down Kanawha River way.

It has been told time and again in the *Beckley Post - Herald*. So, listen my children, and you shall hear anew some of the story of the ghost of Mrs. Zona Heaster Shue, the ill - fated girl of Livesay's Mill, a little settlement in Meadow Bluff District in Greenbrier County.

LIVESAY gets its name from William Livesay. Edward "Trout" Shue, an ex - convict, former resident of Pocahontas County, came to Livesay to work in the blacksmith shop of James Crookshank. There was some talk about Shue but it was a bit subdued.

He was reported to be a widower and a great believer in marriage. Reports said he had married twice before coming to Livesay and that one of his wives had accidentally died on purpose.

IN NOV., 1896, Shue and Zona Heaster were married

Zona's mother lived 14 miles away on the other side of Big Sewell. He and his bride took up housekeeping in the small two - story house that had been the residence of William G. Livesay.

Trouble broke out in that house. One evening when the smithy came home from shop he quarrelled with his wife Zona because there was no meat on the supper table. Result was that he grabbed his wife's face in his strong hands, twisted her neck, killing her!

NEXT MORNING, Shue went to the home of "Aunt Martha" Jones, a woman of color, and asked her to send her boy Anderson Jones up to the Shue house to chop some wood for Mrs. Shue. That was on Saturday, Jan. 22, 1897.

When the boy reached the Shue house he came upon the body of the dead woman. Excitement followed excitement and soon the neighborhood was in an uproar. Shue prepared his wife's body for burial amidst circumstances that aroused suspicion.

Dr. J. M. Knapp had examined the dead woman and from his cursory examination decided she had died from heart failure.

FOUR TIMES the ghost of the dead girl appeared to her mother, Mrs. Heaster. After reporting to county authorities at Lewisburg what Mrs. Heaster said the apparition had told her — that Shue had killed her daughter — the body was ordered exhumed.

This was done and the autopsy proved the girl's neck had been broken! Shue was arrested, tried, convicted and sentenced to the State Penitentiary at Moundsville for the rest of his life. He died there in 1905.

ANDERSON Jones who found the dead Mrs. Shue served as janitor of Mt. Tabor Baptist Church at Lewisburg until he died. I knew Anderson's brother, Reuben Edward Jones, who told me of the Shue affair.

R. E. Jones died Dec. 17, 1962, in the Veterans Administration hospital, Beckley.

Bibliography

Greenbrier Ghost at:

http://en.m.wikipedia.org/wiki/Greenbrier_Ghost

American Society for Psychical Research at:

http://www.aspr.com/

African American Genealogy at:

http://aagenwv.blogspot.com/2006/12/anderson-jones.html

STMU History Media at:

https://stmuhistorymedia.org/

West Virginia Archives and History at:

http://www.wvculture.org/history/crime/shuearticles.html

Dying Words.net at:

http://dyingwords.net/how-a-ghosts-evidence-convicted-a-m
urderer/

Huffington Post at:

https://www.huffpost.com/entry/how-a-ghosts-evidence-con
_b_9252062

Greenbrier Ghost-WV Penitentiary at:

https://wvpentours.com/about/history/articles/the-greenbrier-
ghost/

Murder by Gaslight-Greenbrier Ghost at:

http://www.murderbygaslight.com/2009/12/zona-heaster-shu
e-greenbriar-ghost.html

GRAF WV - The 1897 Schoolhouse Autopsy at:

http://www.grafwv.com/page/content.detail/id/506772/The-1
897-Schoolhouse-Autopsy---the-Greenbrier-Ghost.html?nav
=5004

The Greenbrier Ghost at:

http://www.daffadillies.co.uk/trigger/b720051

The Greenbrier Ghost-Appalachian History at:

http://www.appalachianhistory.net/2018/01/greenbrier-ghost
.html

The Greenbrier Ghost-Zona's Revenge at:

https://www.miamighostchronicles.com/stranger-than-fiction
/the-greenbrier-ghost-zonas-revenge

Whitegate Cemetery at:

http://www.wvgenweb.org/marshall/cemetery/whitegat.htm

Little Things at:

https://www.littlethings.com/the-greenbrier-ghost/2

North House Museum and Greenbrier Historical Society at:

http://www.greenbrierhistorical.org/the-north-house-museu
m.html

Made in United States
North Haven, CT
14 July 2022